THE BEST ADHD MANAGEMENT FOR CHILDREN

Supporting Your Child: A Guide to Managing ADHD

ERIK K. LIPPERT

CONTENTS

INTRODUCTION

Attention Deficit Hyperactivity Disorder (ADHD) is a complex condition that affects millions of children and adults worldwide. It is characterized by symptoms such as impulsivity, hyperactivity, and inattention, which can make it difficult for individuals with ADHD to function in daily life. Despite the challenges that ADHD presents, with the right strategies and support, individuals with ADHD can lead fulfilling lives. This book is a comprehensive guide to understanding and managing ADHD.

This book is designed to provide an in-depth understanding of ADHD, including the signs and symptoms, causes, and risk factors. It also covers the latest research and interventions that can help individuals with ADHD to manage their symptoms and improve their quality of life. Whether you are a parent, caregiver, or an individual with ADHD, this book will provide you with the tools and knowledge you need to understand and manage this condition.

We will explore various strategies and interventions that can help individuals with ADHD to improve their attention, reduce impulsivity, and manage hyperactivity. This includes medication, therapy, behavior management, and educational support, among others. The book will also provide advice on how to cope with the challenges of raising a child with ADHD, as well as tips for adults with ADHD on how to manage their symptoms in the workplace and in their personal lives.

This book is a valuable resource for anyone looking to better understand and manage ADHD. Whether you are new to the topic or have been living with ADHD for a long time, this book will provide you with the information you need to improve your quality of life.

CHAPTER 1

UNDERSTANDING AND TREATING ADHD

Attention-deficit/hyperactivity disorder (ADHD) is a neurodevelopmental disorder that affects both children and adults. It is characterized by symptoms of inattention, impulsivity, and hyperactivity. These symptoms can cause significant difficulties in daily life, including problems with school or work, social interactions, and overall functioning.

The exact cause of ADHD is not known, but it is thought to be a combination of genetic and environmental factors. Research has shown that ADHD is likely to be inherited, with certain genes playing a role in the development of the disorder. Environmental factors, such as prenatal exposure to tobacco smoke or alcohol, may also contribute to the development of ADHD.

ADHD is diagnosed using a combination of criteria from the Diagnostic and Statistical Manual of Mental Disorders (DSM-5) and a thorough evaluation by a healthcare professional. The diagnosis process typically includes a comprehensive medical, psychological, and educational assessment, as well as interviews with parents, teachers, and other caregivers.

There are three subtypes of ADHD: inattentive type, hyperactive-impulsive type, and combined type. The inattentive type is characterized by symptoms of inattention, such as difficulty focusing, forgetfulness, and poor organizational skills. The hyperactive-impulsive type is characterized by symptoms of impulsivity and hyperactivity, such as fidgeting, interrupting others, and acting without thinking. The combined type is characterized by symptoms of both inattention and impulsivity/hyperactivity.

The most common treatment for ADHD is medication, specifically stimulants such as Ritalin and Adderall. These medications work by increasing the levels of certain neurotransmitters in the brain, which can help to improve attention and reduce impulsivity and hyperactivity. However, these medications can have side effects, and it is important for individuals to work closely with their healthcare provider to find the right medication and dosage.

In addition to medication, behavioral therapy is also an effective treatment for ADHD. This type of therapy focuses on teaching individuals with ADHD strategies to manage their symptoms, such as organizational skills, time management, and problem-solving. Behavioral therapy can also help to improve social skills and self-esteem.

Other interventions can also be helpful, such as occupational therapy, which can help with fine motor skills and organizational skills, as well as counseling which can help individuals to understand and cope with their ADHD symptoms, and to improve overall well-being.

It is important to note that ADHD is a lifelong disorder and management of symptoms requires life-long interventions. Therefore, it is important for individuals with ADHD to work with a healthcare provider to develop a treatment plan that is tailored to their specific needs, and to make any necessary adjustments as they go through different stages of life.

In conclusion, ADHD is a neurodevelopmental disorder that affects both children and adults, characterized by symptoms of inattention, impulsivity, and hyperactivity. The exact cause of ADHD is not known, but it is thought to be a combination of genetic and environmental factors. The most common treatment for ADHD is medication, specifically stimulants, along with behavioral therapy, occupational therapy, and counseling. Management of symptoms require life-long interventions, therefore, it is important for individuals with ADHD to work with a healthcare provider to develop a treatment plan that is tailored to their specific needs.

Symptoms of ADHD

Attention Deficit Hyperactivity Disorder (ADHD) is a neurodevelopmental disorder that affects millions of children and adults worldwide. It is characterized by symptoms such as inattention, hyperactivity, and impulsivity. Being aware of the signs and symptoms of ADHD can help individuals and their loved ones seek the appropriate treatment and support.

- Inattention: One of the most common symptoms of ADHD is inattention. Children and adults with ADHD may have difficulty focusing on a task for an extended period of time, may be easily distracted, and may have a hard time following instructions. They may also have trouble organizing their thoughts and tasks and may forget important details.

- Hyperactivity: Hyperactivity is another common symptom of ADHD. Children and adults with this condition may have difficulty sitting still, may fidget or squirm, and may talk excessively. They may also have a hard time engaging in quiet activities and may feel restless.

- Impulsivity: Impulsivity is another symptom of ADHD. Children and adults with this condition may have a hard time waiting their turn, may interrupt others and may act without thinking about the consequences. They may also have trouble controlling their emotions and may act impulsively in response to stress.

- Difficulty with time management: Children and adults with ADHD may have difficulty managing their time effectively. They may procrastinate and have trouble completing tasks, may struggle to meet deadlines, and may have trouble keeping track of important appointments and events.

- Difficulty with self-regulation: Children and adults with ADHD may have difficulty regulating their emotions and behavior. They may have trouble with impulse control, may struggle with anger management, and may have difficulty managing their stress levels.

- Difficulty with social interactions: Children and adults with ADHD may have difficulty with social interactions. They may struggle to make friends, may have trouble understanding social cues and conventions and may have trouble with communication and nonverbal communication.

- Difficulty with academic performance: Children with ADHD may have difficulty with academic performance. They may struggle with reading, writing, and math may have difficulty with memory, and may have difficulty following instructions.

It's worth noting that the symptoms of ADHD can vary from person to person, and some people may only have symptoms of inattention, while others may have symptoms of hyperactivity and impulsivity. Additionally, the symptoms of ADHD may change over time and may be more severe in some situations than in others.

It's important to consult a healthcare professional if you suspect that you or a loved one has ADHD. A comprehensive assessment that includes a medical history, physical examination, and behavioral evaluations can help diagnose ADHD. Once diagnosed, treatment options may include medication, therapy, and/or lifestyle changes.

ADHD is a neurodevelopmental disorder characterized by symptoms such as inattention, hyperactivity, and impulsivity. Symptoms can vary from person to person and may change over time. If you suspect that you or a loved one has ADHD, it's important to seek professional help. With the right treatment and support, individuals with ADHD can lead fulfilling and successful lives.

Causes

Attention Deficit Hyperactivity Disorder (ADHD) is a neurodevelopmental disorder that affects millions of children and adults worldwide. The exact causes of ADHD are not yet fully understood, but research suggests that a combination of genetic, environmental, and neurobiological factors may play a role.

- Genetics: Research suggests that ADHD may be inherited. Studies have shown that individuals with ADHD are more likely to have a family member with the disorder. Furthermore, genetic studies have identified several genes that may be associated with ADHD. However, it's important to note that genetics is not the only cause of ADHD, and many people with the disorder do not have a family history of it.

- Environmental factors: Environmental factors may also play a role in the development of ADHD. Research suggests that certain environmental toxins, such as lead and pesticides, may increase the risk of ADHD. Additionally, prenatal exposure to alcohol, tobacco, and drugs may also be a risk factor for the disorder.

- Brain development and function: Research suggests that certain structural and functional differences in the brain may be associated with ADHD. Studies have shown that certain regions of the brain, including the prefrontal cortex and the basal ganglia, may be underactive in individuals with ADHD. Additionally, research suggests that there may be a dysfunction of the neurotransmitters, which are chemicals in the brain that help transmit signals between nerve cells.

- Trauma: Children who have experienced traumatic events, such as abuse, neglect, or other types of trauma, may be at a higher risk of developing ADHD. Trauma can affect brain development and function, leading to symptoms of ADHD.

-

- Premature birth: Children born prematurely are at a higher risk of developing ADHD. Research suggests that premature birth may be associated with brain injury and other complications that can lead to ADHD.

It's worth noting that the causes of ADHD are complex and multifactorial, and in many cases, the disorder is likely caused by a combination of genetic, environmental, and neurobiological factors. Additionally, the causes of ADHD may be different for different individuals and may change over time.

It's important to seek professional help if you suspect that you or a loved one has ADHD. A comprehensive assessment that includes a medical history, physical examination, and behavioral evaluations can help diagnose ADHD. Once diagnosed, treatment options may include medication, therapy, and/or lifestyle change.

The causes of ADHD are not fully understood, but research suggests that a combination of genetic, environmental, and neurobiological factors may play a role. Factors such as genetics, environmental toxins, brain development and function, trauma, and premature birth may contribute to the disorder. It's important to seek professional help if you suspect that you or a loved one has ADHD and to consider the multiple factors that may be at play. With the right treatment and support, individuals with ADHD can lead fulfilling and successful lives.

Treating ADHD

Treatment for ADHD typically involves a combination of medication, behavioral therapy, and other interventions. The goal of treatment is to manage the symptoms of ADHD and improve functioning in daily life.

Medication is the most common treatment for ADHD. The most commonly prescribed medications for ADHD are stimulants, such as Ritalin and Adderall. These medications work by increasing the levels of certain neurotransmitters in the brain, which can help to improve attention and reduce impulsivity and hyperactivity. They are effective in reducing core symptoms of ADHD such as inattention, impulsivity, and hyperactivity. They may also lead to improvement in academic, social, and occupational areas.

It is important to work closely with a healthcare provider to find the right medication and dosage. The medication may need to be adjusted over time to find the optimal dosage. It is also important to monitor for side effects and any other medication interactions.

Another effective treatment for ADHD is behavioral therapy. This type of therapy focuses on teaching individuals with ADHD strategies to manage their symptoms, such as organizational skills, time management, and problem-solving. Behavioral therapy can also help to improve social skills and self-esteem. Behavioral therapy can be done individually or in a group setting. The therapy can be done by a mental health professional, a teacher, or a specially trained therapist.

Occupational therapy can also be helpful for individuals with ADHD. This type of therapy focuses on fine motor skills, organizational skills, and sensory integration. These interventions can help children with ADHD to be more successful in school and other daily activities.

Counseling can also be beneficial for individuals with ADHD. This type of therapy can help individuals to understand and cope with their ADHD symptoms and to improve overall well-being. Counseling can also be helpful for parents and caregivers, as they may also have to adjust their behavior and expectations to better support their loved ones with ADHD.

There are also other non-traditional interventions that have been found to be effective in treating ADHD such as neurofeedback, mindfulness, and physical exercise. Neurofeedback is a type of therapy that uses real-time displays of brain activity to teach individuals to self-regulate their brain activity. Mindfulness and physical exercise can help to reduce symptoms of ADHD by improving focus, attention, and impulse control.

It is important to note that ADHD is a lifelong disorder, and the management of symptoms requires life-long interventions. Therefore, it is important for individuals with ADHD to work with a healthcare provider to develop a treatment plan that is tailored to their specific needs, and to make any necessary adjustments as they go through different stages of life.

Treatment for ADHD typically involves a combination of medication, behavioral therapy, and other interventions. Medication, specifically stimulants, is the most common treatment for ADHD and it's effective in reducing core symptoms of ADHD such as inattention, impulsivity, and hyperactivity. Behavioral therapy, occupational therapy, counseling, neurofeedback, mindfulness, and physical exercise are also effective in managing symptoms of ADHD. It's important to work closely with a healthcare provider to find the right medication and dosage, and to develop a treatment plan that is tailored to the individual's specific needs. Management of symptoms requires life-long interventions and adjustments as the individual goes through different stages of life.

What to avoid

Attention Deficit Hyperactivity Disorder (ADHD) is characterized by symptoms such as inattention, hyperactivity, and impulsivity. When treating ADHD children, it is important to be aware of certain things that should be avoided in order to ensure that the treatment is effective and safe.

- Overmedication: One of the most common mistakes made when treating ADHD children is overmedication. Stimulant medications such as Ritalin and Adderall are often prescribed to help manage the symptoms of ADHD, but they should be used only as a last resort after other interventions have been tried.

Overmedication can lead to serious side effects such as insomnia, loss of appetite, and even heart problems.

- Ignoring other conditions: ADHD is often accompanied by other conditions such as anxiety, depression, and learning disabilities. It is important to address these conditions in addition to treating ADHD symptoms, as they can exacerbate the symptoms of ADHD.

- Lack of parental involvement: Parental involvement is crucial for the success of any treatment plan for ADHD children. Parents should be involved in the diagnosis, treatment planning, and monitoring of their child's progress. They should also be educated about ADHD and how to manage the symptoms at home.

- Using punishment as a discipline strategy: Children with ADHD are often impulsive and may act out without thinking about the consequences. Punishing them for their behavior can make the situation worse, as it can lead to feelings of frustration, low self-esteem, and even more acting out. Instead, positive reinforcement techniques should be used to encourage good behavior.

- Focusing only on symptoms: While managing symptoms is important, it is also essential to focus on the child's strengths and abilities. Children with ADHD often have unique talents and strengths that should be nurtured and developed.

- Not involving the child in the treatment process: Children with ADHD should be involved in the treatment process and given the opportunity to express their thoughts and feelings. This can help them develop a sense of ownership and responsibility for their own treatment.

Treating ADHD children is a complex process that requires a holistic approach. It is important to avoid overmedication, ignoring other conditions, lack of parental involvement, using punishment as a discipline strategy, focusing only on symptoms, and not involving the child in the treatment process. By taking a holistic approach and involving the child and their family in the treatment process, it is possible to help children with ADHD lead fulfilling and successful lives.

CHAPTER 2

MANAGEMENT OF BEHAVIORAL PROBLEMS

Managing behavioral problems in children with ADHD can be challenging, but there are a variety of strategies that can be used to help improve behavior and promote positive outcomes.

One important strategy is to establish clear and consistent rules and consequences for behavior. This can involve creating a behavior plan that outlines specific behaviors that are expected, as well as the consequences for not following these expectations. It's important to communicate these rules and expectations clearly to the child and to consistently enforce the consequences when the rules are not followed.

Another important strategy is to use positive reinforcement to encourage desired behaviors. This can involve praising the child for following the rules and behaving appropriately, as well as providing rewards for good behavior. It's important to be specific and consistent in the praise and rewards and to use them in a timely manner.

Another way to manage behavioral problems in children with ADHD is to use techniques such as time-out or "token economy" systems to help manage behavior. Time-out involves removing the child from a reinforcing situation for a short period of time in response to an inappropriate behavior. Token economy systems involve giving a child a token or point for each desired behavior, which can be exchanged for a preferred item or activity.

Working with other professionals such as teachers and therapists can also be beneficial in managing behavioral problems in children with

ADHD. Teachers can provide additional support in the classroom and work with the child to develop strategies to improve behavior. Therapists can provide individual or family therapy to help address underlying issues that may be contributing to the child's behavior problems.

It's also important to address any other conditions that may co-occur with ADHD such as anxiety and depression, as they can exacerbate behavioral problems. Medications such as antidepressants may be prescribed in addition to stimulant medication to address these conditions.

It's important to work closely with a healthcare professional to develop a comprehensive treatment plan that addresses both the child's ADHD symptoms and any other conditions that may be present. This may involve medication management, behavioral therapy, and other interventions, such as family therapy.

It's also important to involve the parents and caregivers in the management of behavioral problems in children with ADHD. They can be trained to use the same strategies used in the therapy sessions and to implement them at home as well. This can help to promote consistency and continuity of care, as well as to improve the child's overall functioning.

Managing behavioral problems in children with ADHD can be challenging, but there are a variety of strategies that can be used to help improve behavior and promote positive outcomes. Strategies such as clear and consistent rules and consequences, positive reinforcement, time-out, token economy systems, and working with other professionals can be effective. It's also important to address any other conditions that may co-occur with ADHD and to involve parents and caregivers.

How to minimize these behaviors.

Minimizing behavioral problems in children with ADHD can be challenging, but there are a variety of strategies that can be used to help reduce symptoms and promote positive outcomes.

One important strategy is to establish clear and consistent rules and expectations for behavior. This can involve creating a behavior plan that outlines specific behaviors that are expected, as well as the consequences for not following these expectations. It's important to communicate these rules and expectations clearly to the child and to consistently enforce the consequences when the rules are not followed.

Another important strategy is to use positive reinforcement to encourage desired behaviors. This can involve praising the child for following the rules and behaving appropriately, as well as providing rewards for good behavior. It's important to be specific and consistent in the praise and rewards and to use them in a timely manner.

Another way to minimize behavioral problems in children with ADHD is to provide structure and routine in their daily lives. This can involve creating a daily schedule that includes specific times for homework, meals, and other activities. It's also important to establish a consistent bedtime routine to help the child wind down in the evening.

Working with other professionals such as teachers and therapists can also be beneficial in minimizing behavioral problems in children with ADHD. Teachers can provide additional support in the classroom and work with the child to develop strategies to improve behavior. Therapists can provide individual or family therapy to help address underlying issues that may be contributing to the child's behavior problems.

Parent training can be helpful in minimizing behavioral problems in children with ADHD. The parent can learn strategies to manage their child's behavior, improve communication, and how work with the child to prevent problematic behavior.

It's also important to address any other conditions that may co-occur with ADHD such as anxiety and depression, as they can exacerbate behavioral problems. Medications such as antidepressants may be prescribed in addition to stimulant medication to address these conditions.

Physical activity and regular exercise can be helpful in minimizing behavioral problems in children with ADHD. Exercise can help to improve focus and attention, as well as reduce hyperactivity and impulsivity. Encouraging the child to participate in sports or other physical activities can be beneficial.

It's important to note that children with ADHD may need a different approach than other children, and it's important to work closely with a healthcare professional to develop a comprehensive treatment plan that addresses both the child's ADHD symptoms and any other conditions that may be present. This may involve medication management, behavioral therapy, and other interventions, such as family therapy.

In conclusion, minimizing behavioral problems in children with ADHD can be challenging, but there are a variety of strategies that can be used to help reduce symptoms and promote positive outcomes. Strategies such as clear and consistent rules and expectations, positive reinforcement, providing structure and routine, working with other professionals, parent training, addressing co-occurring conditions, regular exercise, and physical activity can be effective. It's also important to work closely with a healthcare professional to develop a comprehensive treatment plan that addresses both the child's

ADHD symptoms and any other conditions that may be present.

Managing a child's emotional control can be a challenging task for parents and caregivers. Children, especially those with conditions such as ADHD and autism, may have difficulty regulating their emotions and may struggle with impulsivity and hyperactivity. However, with the right strategies, children can learn to manage their emotions and develop healthy coping mechanisms.

- Teach emotional vocabulary: Children need to be able to identify and label their emotions in order to understand and manage them. Teach your child the names of different emotions and help them understand what each emotion feels like in their body. This will give them the tools they need to communicate their feelings to you and others.

- Encourage mindfulness: Mindfulness practices such as deep breathing, yoga, and meditation can help children to focus their attention and become more aware of their emotions. Encourage your child to take deep breaths when they are feeling overwhelmed and to focus on the present moment.

- Model healthy coping mechanisms: Children learn by example, so it's important to model healthy coping mechanisms for them. Show them how to take a break when they are feeling stressed, how to talk about their feelings, and how to practice self-care.

- Encourage physical activity: Physical activity is a great way to release pent-up energy and emotions. Encourage your child to participate in sports, dance, or other physical activities that they enjoy.

- Provide positive reinforcement: Positive reinforcement is a powerful tool for shaping behavior. Reward your child when they display self-control and emotional regulation.

- Provide structure and routine: Children with difficulty regulating their emotions may benefit from a structured and predictable routine. This will help them to feel more secure and to know what to expect.

- Seek professional help: If your child is having difficulty managing their emotions, it may be helpful to seek professional help. A mental health professional, such as a psychologist or counselor, can work with you and your child to develop strategies for managing emotions.

- Be patient: Managing emotions is a process that takes time. Be patient with your child and remember that they are still learning.

Managing children's emotional control can be challenging, but with the right strategies, children can learn to manage their emotions and develop healthy coping mechanisms. Encourage children to use emotional vocabulary, practice mindfulness, model healthy coping mechanisms, encourage physical activity, provide positive reinforcement, provide structure and routine, seek professional help and be patient. With patience, understanding, and consistent support, children can develop the skills they need to manage their emotions and lead fulfilling lives.

CHAPTER 3

INSTRUCTIONAL STRATEGIES AND SUPPORT FOR CHILDREN WITH ADHD

Managing children with ADHD in the classroom can be challenging, but there are a variety of instructional strategies that can be used to help improve their academic performance and behavior.

One important strategy is to provide a structured and predictable classroom environment. This can involve creating a daily schedule that includes specific times for academic activities, as well as breaks for physical activity and movement. It's also important to establish clear and consistent rules and expectations for behavior and to communicate these rules clearly to the child and other students.

Another important strategy is to use a variety of teaching methods to help engage children with ADHD. This can involve using hands-on activities, visual aids, and technology to help keep the child's attention and interest. It's also important to provide opportunities for the child to move and be active during the day, as this can help to reduce hyperactivity and impulsivity.

Another instructional strategy is to provide individualized instruction that meets the child's specific needs. This can involve working with the child one-on-one or in small groups to provide extra support and guidance. It's also important to monitor the child's progress and to make adjustments to the instruction as needed.

Another strategy is to use positive reinforcement to encourage desired behaviors and academic performance. This can involve praising the child for following the rules and behaving appropriately, as well as providing rewards for good behavior and academic performance.

It's also important to work closely with other professionals such as school psychologists or behavioral therapists to develop a comprehensive treatment plan that addresses both the child's ADHD symptoms and any other conditions that may be present. This may involve medication management, behavioral therapy, and other interventions, such as family therapy.

It's also important to involve the parents and caregivers in the management of children with ADHD in the classroom. They can be informed about the strategies used in the classroom and implement them at home as well. This can help to promote consistency and continuity of care, as well as to improve the child's overall functioning.

Managing children with ADHD in the classroom can be challenging, but there are a variety of instructional strategies that can be used to help improve their academic performance and behavior. Strategies such as providing a structured and predictable classroom environment, using a variety of teaching methods, providing individualized instruction, positive reinforcement, working with other professionals, and involving parents and caregivers can be effective. It's also important to work closely with a healthcare professional to develop a comprehensive treatment plan that addresses both the child's ADHD symptoms and any other conditions that may be present.

Attention-deficit/hyperactivity disorder (ADHD) is a neurodevelopmental disorder that affects children and can continue into adulthood. Supporting children with ADHD can be challenging, but there are several strategies that can be effective.

Establish a routine and structure: Children with ADHD often have difficulty with organization and time management. Establishing a daily routine and providing clear expectations can help them stay on task and manage their time more effectively.

Provide positive reinforcement: Children with ADHD may struggle with impulsivity and may not respond well to traditional forms of punishment. Instead, focus on positive reinforcement for good behavior. Praise, rewards, and other forms of positive feedback can be very effective in motivating children with ADHD.

Address academic needs: Many children with ADHD struggle academically. Special accommodations, such as extra time on tests, may be necessary to help them succeed. In addition, providing a quiet work area and breaking assignments into smaller chunks can also be helpful.

Help with social skills: Children with ADHD may struggle with social interactions. Teaching them how to understand and express emotions, how to start and maintain conversations, and how to understand nonverbal cues can be beneficial.

Encourage physical activity: Children with ADHD often have a lot of energy to burn. Encouraging regular physical activity, such as sports or other physical activities, can help them channel that energy in a positive way.

Provide medication management: Medications such as stimulants can be effective in managing symptoms of ADHD, but they must be prescribed and monitored by a doctor.

Provide emotional support: Children with ADHD may have difficulty with self-esteem and may feel frustrated or overwhelmed by their symptoms. Emotional support, such as regular counseling and therapy, can be beneficial in helping them develop coping strategies and build resilience.

Work with the family: ADHD affects not just the child but the whole family. Parents, caregivers, and siblings may need support and education in understanding the disorder and how to provide the best support for the child.

Collaborate with school: Schools can play a vital role in supporting children with ADHD, by providing appropriate accommodations, such as preferential seating, extra time for tests, and modifications to the curriculum. Collaboration between the family, doctor, and school can help ensure that the child receives the support they need to succeed.

Be patient and consistent: Supporting a child with ADHD can be challenging, and progress may be slow. It's important to be patient and consistent in your approach and to remember that every child is unique and may respond differently to different interventions.

Getting the attention of students in a classroom can be a challenging task for teachers. With distractions such as technology, social media, and other forms of entertainment, it can be difficult to keep students engaged and focused on the task at hand. However, there are a number of strategies that teachers can use to get and keep students' attention.

Start with a hook: The first few minutes of class are crucial for capturing students' attention. Use a "hook" to engage students and make them curious about the topic. This could be a question, a problem, or a real-world example that relates to the lesson.

Use active learning strategies: Active learning strategies, such as group work, discussions, and hands-on activities, can help to keep students engaged and focused. By actively participating in the learning process, students are more likely to pay attention and retain information.

Use variety in instruction: Students can easily lose interest if the instruction is monotonous. Use a variety of teaching methods to keep students engaged, such as lectures, videos, images, and interactive games.

Use positive reinforcement: Positive reinforcement is a powerful tool for shaping behavior. Reward students when they display good attention and focus and recognize their efforts.

Set clear expectations: Make sure that students understand what is expected of them in terms of attention and behavior. Clearly communicate expectations and consequences for not following them.

Give regular breaks: Long periods of sitting and listening can be tiring for students. Giving regular breaks can help to refresh their attention and energy.

Address distractions: Be aware of the distractions in your classroom and address them as needed. For example, if students are having trouble focusing because of noise from the hallway, consider closing the door or using white noise to reduce distraction.

Use technology effectively: Technology can be both a distraction and a tool for engagement. Use technology in ways that support learning, such as interactive games and videos that relate to the lesson.

Personalize instruction: Get to know your students and their interests and tailor instruction to their needs.

Show enthusiasm: Students are more likely to pay attention to a teacher who is passionate about the subject matter. Show enthusiasm for the material and your students will be more likely to follow suit.

Getting and keeping students' attention is a critical aspect of teaching. Using strategies such as starting with a hook, using active learning strategies, using variety in instruction, using positive reinforcement, setting clear expectations, giving regular breaks, addressing distractions, using technology effectively, personalizing instruction, and showing enthusiasm can help teachers to capture and maintain students' attention in the classroom. With the right approach, teachers can create an environment where students are engaged, motivated, and excited to learn.

Overall, supporting a child with ADHD requires a comprehensive approach that addresses the child's unique needs. With the right support and accommodations, children with ADHD can thrive and reach their full potential.

CHAPTER 4

TOP STRATEGIES THAT WORK

Attention Deficit Hyperactivity Disorder (ADHD) is a neurodevelopmental disorder that affects both children and adults. It is characterized by symptoms such as difficulty paying attention, impulsivity, and hyperactivity. Managing ADHD can be challenging, but there are several strategies and methods that have been shown to be effective.

- Medication: Stimulant medications such as Ritalin and Adderall are commonly prescribed to manage symptoms of ADHD. These medications work by increasing the levels of certain neurotransmitters in the brain, which can help improve attention and reduce impulsivity and hyperactivity. Medication can be an effective treatment for many individuals with ADHD, but it is important to work closely with a healthcare provider to find the right medication and dosage.

- Behavioral therapy: Behavioral therapy is another effective treatment for ADHD. This may include techniques such as positive reinforcement, goal setting, and parent training to help manage and improve behavior. For example, a child with ADHD may be rewarded for staying on task and completing homework, while a parent may be taught how to use positive reinforcement to encourage good behavior. Behavioral therapy can be done individually or in a group setting and can be an effective way to manage symptoms of ADHD.

- Organization and planning: One of the biggest challenges for individuals with ADHD is staying organized and on task. Strategies such as using a planner, breaking tasks into smaller steps, and setting reminders can help individuals with ADHD stay on track and manage time more effectively. For example, breaking a large project into smaller tasks and setting deadlines for each task can make it easier to stay focused and avoid procrastination.

- Exercise and healthy lifestyle: Regular physical activity and a healthy diet can help improve symptoms of ADHD. Exercise has been shown to increase the levels of certain neurotransmitters in the brain, which can help improve attention and reduce impulsivity and hyperactivity. Eating a healthy diet that is rich in fruits, vegetables, and whole grains can also provide essential nutrients that are important for brain function.

- Support: Support from family, friends, and a therapist or counselor can be beneficial for individuals with ADHD. Having a supportive network of people who understand and can provide guidance and encouragement can make it easier to manage the symptoms of ADHD. Therapy can also be an effective way to work through any emotional or behavioral issues that may be related to ADHD.

- Mindfulness and meditation: Mindfulness practices such as meditation and yoga can help individuals with ADHD improve focus and reduce impulsivity. These practices teach individuals to focus on the present moment and become more aware of their thoughts and feelings. This can help individuals with ADHD stay on task and avoid distractions, as well as reduce feelings of anxiety and stress.

- Counseling and therapy: Therapy can help individuals with ADHD learn ways to manage their symptoms, set goals, and improve their overall quality of life. Therapy can also help individuals with ADHD work through any emotional or behavioral issues that may be related to the disorder. Counseling and therapy can be done individually or in a group setting and can be an effective way to manage symptoms of ADHD.

It's important to note that ADHD is a complex disorder and treatment plans need to be tailored to the individual. A combination of different strategies and methods may be more effective than one single approach. This may include a combination of medication, behavioral therapy, and lifestyle changes. It is also important to work closely with a healthcare provider to find the right treatment plan.

ADHD is a common and challenging disorder, but there are several strategies and methods that have been shown to be effective in managing symptoms. Medication, behavioral therapy, organization and planning, exercise and a healthy lifestyle, support, mindfulness and meditation, and counseling and therapy are all.

Working memory is an essential cognitive function that allows us to temporarily store and manipulate information. It plays a crucial role in a wide range of cognitive processes such as learning, problem-solving, and decision-making. Weakness in working memory can have a significant impact on an individual's ability to perform these tasks and can lead to difficulties in academic and occupational settings.

Working memory weakness can manifest in a variety of ways, including difficulty remembering instructions, trouble following multi-step directions, and difficulty with tasks that require mental manipulation of information, such as math problems. Individuals with working memory weakness may also experience difficulty with attention and organization.

There are a number of different factors that can contribute to working memory weakness. Some individuals may have a genetic predisposition to working memory weakness, while others may develop weakness due to brain injury or illness. Additionally, environmental factors such as stress, lack of sleep, and poor nutrition can also affect working memory.

Support for individuals with working memory weakness can take many forms. One effective strategy is to provide individuals with strategies to improve their working memory. This can include teaching individuals to break down complex tasks into smaller, more manageable steps and providing them with mnemonic devices to help them remember information.

Another important aspect of support is to provide accommodations that can help to reduce the impact of working memory weakness on an individual's ability to perform tasks. This can include providing extra time for completing tasks, breaking down complex tasks into smaller steps, and providing visual aids to help individuals organize information.

There are also many tools and apps available that can be used to help individuals with working memory weaknesses. These tools can include memory games, flashcards, and other exercises that are designed to help improve working memory.

Furthermore, Medication can also be used as a form of support for individuals with working memory weakness. Medications such as stimulants can help to improve attention and focus, which can in turn improve working memory. However, it is important to note that medication should always be used in conjunction with other forms of support, such as therapy and accommodations.

In conclusion, working memory weakness can have a significant impact on an individual's ability to perform a wide range of cognitive tasks. However, with the right support, individuals with working memory weakness can learn to manage their symptoms and improve their ability to perform tasks. This support can take many forms, including teaching strategies to improve working memory, providing accommodations, using tools and apps, and medication if needed. It is important to work closely with a professional such as a neuropsychologist or an occupational therapist to develop an individualized plan that addresses the unique needs of each person.

Memory Improving Strategies

Memory is an essential cognitive function that plays a crucial role in our daily lives. It enables us to store and retrieve information and helps us to learn and make sense of the world around us. However, memory can decline with age, and some people may experience memory problems due to neurological conditions or injuries.

Fortunately, there are several strategies that can help to improve and maintain a memory.

- Exercise: Regular physical activity has been shown to improve memory and cognitive function. Exercise increases blood flow to the brain, which can help to nourish and protect brain cells. It also helps to release chemicals called growth factors that promote the growth of new brain cells. Exercise can also help to reduce stress and anxiety, which can negatively impact memory.

- Sleep: Sleep plays a crucial role in memory consolidation, the process by which information is transferred from short-term to long-term memory. Studies have shown that people who get a good night's sleep are better able to remember information than those who do not. Getting adequate sleep can also help to reduce fatigue and improve focus, which can make it easier to pay attention and absorb new information.

- Learning new things: Keeping the brain active by learning new things can help to improve memory. This could be anything from learning a new language to taking up a new hobby. Studies have shown that people who engage in activities that challenge their brain, such as solving puzzles or playing memory games, have a better memory than those who do not.

- Memory techniques: There are several memory techniques that can be used to improve memory. One of the most popular techniques is the "method of loci," which involves creating mental images of objects or information and placing them in specific locations. Another technique is the "peg method," which involves creating a memorable image or word that represents a piece of information. These techniques can make it easier to remember information and can be particularly useful for remembering lists or sequences.

- Diet: Eating a healthy diet that is rich in fruits, vegetables, and omega-3 fatty acids can help to improve memory. These foods are high in antioxidants and nutrients that are important for brain health. Studies have also shown that people who eat a Mediterranean diet, which is high in fish, fruits, and vegetables, have a lower risk of developing memory problems.

- Social engagement: Social engagement is another important strategy for improving memory. Studies have shown that people who have strong social connections and engage in social activities have a better memory than those who do not. Socializing with friends and family can also help to reduce stress and anxiety, which can negatively impact memory.

- Stress management: Stress can have a negative impact on memory by releasing chemicals that can damage brain cells. Managing stress through activities such as yoga, meditation, or deep breathing can help to reduce stress and improve memory.

- Medications: Some medications can help to improve memory by increasing the levels of certain neurotransmitters in the brain. These include cholinesterase inhibitors, which are used to treat Alzheimer's disease, and donepezil, rivastigmine, and galantamine, which can be used to improve memory and cognitive function in people with mild to moderate dementia.

It is worth noting that some strategies may work better for some people than others and that it is important to find what works best for you. A combination of different strategies such as exercising, eating well, socializing, and practicing memory techniques can be an effective way to improve memory. It's also important to consult with a healthcare provider if you have concerns about your memory or if you have a medical condition that may be affecting your memory.

Memory is a vital cognitive function and plays an important role in our daily lives.

CHAPTER 5

ACADEMIC SUPPORT IN READING AND WRITING

Children with Attention-Deficit/Hyperactivity Disorder (ADHD) often face a range of academic difficulties. These can include difficulty with attention, organization, memory, and impulsivity.

Attention difficulties can make it hard for children with ADHD to focus on their schoolwork, especially during lectures or when completing independent work. They may have trouble paying attention to details, which can lead to errors on assignments and tests.

Organization difficulties can make it hard for children with ADHD to keep track of their materials and assignments, leading to lost homework and forgotten deadlines. This can also make it hard for them to plan and prioritize their time effectively.

Memory difficulties can make it hard for children with ADHD to recall information they have learned, which can lead to poor performance on tests and quizzes.

Impulsivity can lead to difficulties with impulse control, which can result in interrupting others, blurting out answers, and difficulty waiting their turn. These behaviors can disrupt the classroom and negatively impact learning.

Additionally, children with ADHD may have difficulty with self-regulation, which can make it hard for them to manage their emotions and behavior. This can lead to difficulties with social interactions, which can negatively impact their relationships with peers and teachers.

Overall, children with ADHD face a range of academic difficulties that can impact their performance in school and their ability to succeed academically. It's important for teachers and parents to work together to provide support and accommodations to help these children succeed.

Common reading problems

Attention-deficit/hyperactivity disorder (ADHD) affects children, teens, and adults. One of the most common symptoms of ADHD is difficulty with attention and focus, which can impact a child's ability to read effectively.

Children with ADHD often have a hard time sitting still and focusing on a task for an extended period of time, which can make reading a challenge. They may also have difficulty understanding and remembering what they read, as well as difficulty with decoding and comprehension.

One of the most common reading problems seen in children with ADHD is difficulty with decoding, which is the ability to translate written words into spoken words. Children with ADHD may struggle to sound out words and may have difficulty with phonics and phonological awareness. This can make it difficult for them to read new words and can lead to frustration and a lack of confidence in their reading abilities.

Another common reading problem seen in children with ADHD is difficulty with comprehension. Children with ADHD may have trouble understanding what they read, as well as retaining information from what they read. This can make it difficult for them to follow along with a story or to answer questions about what they have read.

Additionally, children with ADHD may have difficulty with attention and focus, which can make it hard for them to stay on task and engaged while reading. They may become easily distracted and may have trouble completing a book or reading assignment. This can lead to frustration and a lack of progress in reading.

There are several strategies that can be used to help children with ADHD overcome these reading problems. One of the most effective strategies is to break down reading into smaller, manageable chunks. This can help children with ADHD stay focused and engaged and can make it easier for them to understand and remember what they have read.

Another strategy that can be helpful is to use visual aids and other tools, such as flashcards and graphic organizers, to help children with ADHD understand and retain the information they are reading.

It is also important to work with a teacher or reading specialist who is trained in working with children with ADHD. They can provide targeted instruction and support to help children with ADHD improve their reading skills.

Finally, it is important to work with a physician or other healthcare professional to ensure that the child's ADHD is properly managed. Medication and other interventions can help children with ADHD improve their focus and attention, which can in turn improve their reading abilities.

Children with ADHD often experience common reading problems such as difficulty with decoding, comprehension, attention, and focus. But with proper strategies, targeted instruction and support, and proper management of ADHD, children with ADHD can improve their reading skills and become successful readers.

Support to reading and write

Attention-Deficit/Hyperactivity Disorder (ADHD) affects millions of children and can make it challenging for them to learn and excel academically. One of the most challenging areas for children with ADHD is learning to read and write. However, with the right support, children with ADHD can learn to read and write and succeed academically.

One of the most important things parents can do to support their child with ADHD in reading and writing is to create a positive learning environment. This means creating a quiet, organized, and distraction-free space for your child to study. It's also important to establish a consistent routine for homework and study time to help your child develop good study habits.

Another important aspect is to provide appropriate accommodations for your child's learning needs. Children with ADHD may require extra time to complete assignments, or may benefit from using a computer to type assignments instead of writing by hand. Many students with ADHD benefit from using visual aids like flashcards, pictures, and diagrams to help them understand and retain information.

In addition to providing accommodations, parents can also use specific teaching methods to help their child with ADHD learn to read and write. For example, many children with ADHD benefit from multisensory teaching methods, which use a combination of visual, auditory, and kinesthetic cues to help children learn. This can include using flashcards, manipulatives, and other hands-on materials to help children learn to read and write.

It's also important for parents to work closely with their child's teacher to ensure that their child is receiving the appropriate support in the classroom. Teachers can provide additional support in the form of small group instruction, one-on-one tutoring, or other specialized instruction to help children with ADHD learn to read and write.

Additionally, parents should consider seeking out additional support from a specialist, such as an occupational therapist or reading specialist. These professionals can provide targeted interventions and strategies to help children with ADHD learn to read and write more effectively.

Finally, parents need to remember that children with ADHD may need extra time and patience when learning to read and write. Children with ADHD may struggle more than their peers, but with the right support, they can learn to read and write and achieve academic success.

Children with ADHD face unique challenges when learning to read and write. However, with the right support, accommodations, and teaching methods, children with ADHD can succeed academically. Parents play a crucial role in supporting their child's learning and development. It's important for parents to work closely with teachers and specialists to provide the appropriate support and accommodations to help their child learn to read and write effectively.

Tips for a great reader

Children with ADHD can improve their reading skills and become successful readers. In this article, we will discuss some reading tips for children with ADHD to help them overcome common reading problems and improve their reading abilities.

Break reading into smaller chunks: Children with ADHD often have difficulty sitting still and focusing on a task for an extended period of time. To help them stay engaged and focused, it is important to break down reading into smaller, manageable chunks. This can be done by reading a few pages at a time, or by taking frequent breaks to allow the child to move around and refocus.

Use visual aids: Children with ADHD often have difficulty understanding and retaining information from what they read. Using visual aids, such as flashcards, graphic organizers, and illustrations can help children better understand and remember the information they are reading.

Use multisensory approach: Multisensory approach can help children with ADHD to stay engaged and focused and can make it easier for them to understand and remember what they have read. This approach includes reading aloud, using their finger to point out words, and allowing them to read with a buddy.

Provide targeted instruction: Children with ADHD may struggle with specific reading skills, such as decoding or comprehension. It is important to work with a teacher or reading specialist who is trained in working with children with ADHD to provide targeted instruction and support to help the child improve these skills.

Make reading fun: Children with ADHD may become easily bored or discouraged when reading. To keep them engaged and motivated, it is important to make reading fun. This can be done by choosing books that are interesting and age-appropriate, and by incorporating games and activities that relate to the book being read.

Encourage independent reading: Encourage children with ADHD to read independently as much as possible. Independent reading allows children to read at their own pace and to choose books that they are interested in. This can help them develop a love of reading and can also improve their reading fluency and comprehension.

Work with a healthcare professional: It is important to work with a physician or other healthcare professional to ensure that the child's ADHD is properly managed. Medication and other interventions can help children with ADHD improve their focus and attention, which can in turn improve their reading abilities.

Reading can be a challenge for children with ADHD, but with the right strategies and support, they can overcome common reading problems and become successful readers. Breaking reading into smaller chunks, using visual aids, multisensory approach, providing targeted instruction, making reading fun, encouraging independent reading, and working with healthcare professionals are some effective strategies that can help children with ADHD improve their reading skills. It is important to remember that every child is unique and what works for one child may not work for another, so it's essential to be patient and to work closely with the child and the appropriate professionals to find the best approach.

Strategies for building writing skills

Writing can be a challenging task for children with ADHD, as it requires sustained attention and focus. However, there are several strategies that can help to improve their writing skills.

Break writing tasks into smaller chunks: Rather than expecting a child to write a long essay in one sitting, break the task into smaller chunks, such as brainstorming, outlining, writing the introduction, and so on. This will make the task more manageable and less overwhelming.

Use graphic organizers: Graphic organizers, such as flowcharts and mind maps, can help children with ADHD organize their thoughts and ideas before they begin writing.

Encourage freewriting: Freewriting is a technique where children are asked to write whatever comes to mind without worrying about grammar, punctuation, or spelling. This can help to get their creative juices flowing and make the writing process less stressful.

Use technology: There are several software programs and apps that can help children with ADHD to improve their writing skills. For example, word prediction software can help to reduce spelling errors and improve typing speed, while text-to-speech software can help children to hear their writing and make revisions.

Provide feedback: Give children with ADHD specific, constructive feedback on their writing. This will help them to understand what they are doing well and where they need to improve.

Remind them to take breaks: Children with ADHD may have a hard time focusing for long periods of time. Encourage them to take short breaks during the writing process to help them stay refreshed and focused.

It's important to remember that every child is different, so it may take some trial and error to find the strategies that work best for your child with ADHD. With patience and support, your child can develop their writing skills and become a confident writer.

CHAPTER 6

SYSTEM AND EDUCATIONAL RIGHT OF SUPPORT AT SCHOOL

Children with ADHD have the right to receive support in school to help them succeed academically and socially. This support is provided through a process known as the "system of support," which is designed to meet the unique needs of each child with ADHD.

- Identification and assessment: The first step in the system of support is to identify and assess children with ADHD. This typically involves a comprehensive evaluation by a team of professionals, including a physician, a psychologist, and a special education teacher. This evaluation will help to determine the specific needs of the child and how best to support them in the classroom.

- Individualized Education Program (IEP): Once a child with ADHD has been identified, an Individualized Education Program (IEP) is developed. An IEP is a document that outlines the child's specific needs and the supports and services that will be provided to meet those needs. The IEP is reviewed and revised annually to ensure that it continues to meet the child's evolving needs.

- Accommodations and modifications: Children with ADHD may require accommodations and modifications to the classroom and testing environments to help them succeed. These may include things like extra time on tests, preferential seating, and the use of assistive technology.

- Behavioral interventions: Children with ADHD often struggle with impulse control and attention, so behavior interventions can be a key component of their support in the classroom. This can include positive reinforcement, token economies, and social skills training.

- Collaboration and communication: The success of the system of support for children with ADHD depends on collaboration and communication among all the stakeholders involved, including the child, parents, teachers, and other school staff. Regular meetings should be held to review the child's progress, identify areas of concern, and make any necessary adjustments to the support plan.

- Inclusive education: Children with ADHD have the right to be educated in inclusive classrooms alongside their non-disabled peers. This approach has been shown to be beneficial for children with ADHD, as it provides them with opportunities to learn from and interact with their peers.

The system of support is an essential tool for ensuring that children with ADHD receive the support they need to succeed in school. It involves identification and assessment, individualized education programs, accommodations and modifications, behavioral interventions, collaboration and communication, and inclusive education. With the appropriate support and accommodations, children with ADHD can reach their full potential and succeed academically, socially, and emotionally.

What about IDEA?

The Individuals with Disabilities Education Act (IDEA) is a federal law that ensures that students with disabilities have the same opportunities to receive a free and appropriate public education as their non-disabled peers. This includes ensuring that students with disabilities are not disciplined differently from their non-disabled peers.

- Positive Behavioral Interventions and Supports (PBIS): IDEA encourages the use of positive behavioral interventions and supports (PBIS) to address behavior problems in students with disabilities. PBIS is a proactive, data-driven approach that focuses on teaching positive behavior and providing consistent consequences for misbehavior.

- Functional Behavioral Assessment (FBA): Before disciplinary action is taken against a student with a disability, a functional behavioral assessment (FBA) must be conducted to determine the reason for the student's misbehavior. An FBA is a process that looks at the relationship between a student's behavior and the environment in which it occurs. The information gathered during an FBA is used to develop a behavior intervention plan (BIP) to address the student's misbehavior.

- Behavior Intervention Plan (BIP): A BIP is a plan that outlines specific strategies to address a student's misbehavior. The BIP should include positive strategies to teach appropriate behavior, as well as consequences for misbehavior that are consistent and predictable.

- Least Restrictive Environment (LRE): IDEA requires that students with disabilities be educated in the least restrictive environment (LRE) appropriate for their needs. This means that students with disabilities should be placed in the most inclusive setting possible, such as a general education classroom, before being considered for a more restrictive setting, such as a special education classroom or a residential facility.

- Due process: IDEA provides students with disabilities and their families with certain due process rights, including the right to an impartial hearing, the right to an attorney, and the right to appeal a decision. If a student with a disability is facing disciplinary action, the student and their family should be informed of their due process rights.

- Collaboration: IDEA encourages collaboration among all stakeholders, including parents, teachers, and administrators, to ensure that students with disabilities are not disciplined differently from their non-disabled peers. Regular meetings should be held to review the student's progress, identify areas of concern, and make any necessary adjustments to the support plan.

It's important to note that disciplinary action against students with disabilities should be a last resort after all other strategies have been exhausted. The goal should always be to teach appropriate behavior and support the student's success in the least restrictive environment possible. With appropriate support, students with disabilities can learn to manage their behavior and succeed academically and socially.

There are several systems that can be used to train children with ADHD to improve their behavior and academic performance.

- Positive Behavioral Interventions and Supports (PBIS): PBIS is a proactive, data-driven approach that focuses on teaching positive behavior and providing consistent consequences for misbehavior. It involves setting clear expectations for behavior and providing positive reinforcement for meeting those expectations.

- Cognitive Behavioral Therapy (CBT): CBT is a form of therapy that helps children with ADHD to change negative thought patterns and behaviors. It involves teaching children to identify and challenge negative thoughts, develop coping strategies, and set goals for themselves.

- Social skills training: Children with ADHD may have difficulty with social interactions, so social skills training can be beneficial. This type of training teaches children to appropriate social behaviors, such as making eye contact, taking turns in conversation, and understanding social cues.

- Mindfulness training: Mindfulness training can help children with ADHD to improve their attention and focus. This involves teaching children techniques such as deep breathing, meditation, and yoga to help them stay calm and focused.

- Parent training: Parents of children with ADHD can benefit from training programs that teach them how to provide effective support and guidance to their children. This can include strategies for managing behavior, setting limits, and providing positive reinforcement.

- Medication: Medication can be used to help control the symptoms of ADHD, such as impulsivity and hyperactivity. However, it should be used in conjunction with other interventions, such as therapy and behavior management techniques.

It's important to note that every child is different and may respond differently to different interventions. It may take some trial and error to find the systems that work best for your child with ADHD. With patience and support, your child can learn to manage their symptoms and succeed academically and socially.

CHAPTER 7

UNDERSTANDING THE OUTCOME OF CHILDREN WITH ADHD

Understanding the outcome of children with ADHD is essential for providing the appropriate support and interventions to help them succeed academically, socially, and emotionally.

- Academic performance: Children with ADHD often struggle with attention and organization, which can affect their academic performance. However, with the appropriate support and accommodations, such as extra time on tests and the use of assistive technology, children with ADHD can improve their academic performance.

- Social skills: Children with ADHD may also struggle with social interactions and have difficulty understanding social cues. Social skills training can help children with ADHD to improve their social interactions and build positive relationships.

- Emotional regulation: Children with ADHD often have difficulty regulating their emotions, which can lead to impulsivity and impulsive behavior. Mindfulness training and cognitive behavioral therapy can help children with ADHD to learn to regulate their emotions and manage their behavior.

- Self-esteem: Children with ADHD may struggle with low self-esteem due to their difficulties in academic and social areas. It's important to provide positive reinforcement and support to build their self-esteem, as well as to address any negative thoughts they may have about themselves.

- Family support: Families of children with ADHD may also experience stress and strain, it's important to provide support and resources to help families to cope with the challenges of raising a child with ADHD.

- Long-term outcomes: Children with ADHD are at risk for long-term negative outcomes, such as academic underachievement, social isolation, and behavioral problems, if their symptoms are not effectively managed. With appropriate support and interventions, children with ADHD can overcome these risks and lead successful lives.

Remember that every child with ADHD is different and may have unique needs. A comprehensive approach that includes a variety of interventions, such as behavior management, therapy, and medication, can help to improve the outcome for children with ADHD. With patience, understanding, and the right support, children with ADHD can reach their full potential and lead successful lives.

How to maximize these outcomes.

Maximizing the outcome for children with Attention Deficit Hyperactivity Disorder (ADHD) requires a comprehensive approach that includes a variety of interventions and support. Early identification and intervention, multimodal treatment, consistency, and structure are key elements that can help children with ADHD to reach their full potential.

- Early identification and intervention: The earlier a child is diagnosed with ADHD and receives appropriate interventions, the better their outcome is likely to be. Parents and caregivers should be aware of the signs and symptoms of ADHD and seek evaluation from a qualified healthcare professional if they suspect their child may have the disorder. Once a child has been diagnosed with ADHD, interventions can be started as soon as possible.

- Multimodal treatment: A combination of interventions is more effective than a single approach. This includes medication, therapy, behavior management, and educational support. Medication can help to control symptoms such as impulsivity and hyperactivity, while therapy can help children to learn coping strategies and improve social skills. Behavioral management techniques can help children to learn appropriate behaviors, while educational support can help to improve academic performance.

- Consistency and structure: Children with ADHD benefit from a consistent and structured environment. This includes setting clear rules and expectations, using visual aids, providing a quiet place to work, and breaking down tasks into smaller steps. Consistency in routines and structure can help children with ADHD to feel more secure and less overwhelmed.

- Parental training: Parents and caregivers play a crucial role in the outcome of children with ADHD. Parental training programs can teach parents how to provide effective support and guidance to their children. This can include strategies for managing behavior, setting limits, and providing positive reinforcement.

CHAPTER 8

TOP GUIDE TO PARENTAL CARE OF CHILDREN WITH ADHD

As a parent, it can be challenging to raise a child with Attention Deficit Hyperactivity Disorder (ADHD). However, with the right strategies and support, parents can help their children with ADHD to reach their full potential. In this article, we will discuss the top guide to parental care for children with ADHD.

Understand the condition: The first step in providing effective care for a child with ADHD is to understand the condition. This includes learning about the signs and symptoms, as well as the causes and risk factors for ADHD. Understanding the condition can help parents to better recognize and respond to their child's needs.

Seek professional help: Children with ADHD often require a variety of interventions, including medication, therapy, behavior management, and educational support. Seeking the help of a healthcare professional can ensure that your child receives the appropriate treatments and services.

Create a structured environment: Children with ADHD benefit from a structured and consistent environment. This includes setting clear rules and expectations, using visual aids, providing a quiet place to work, and breaking down tasks into smaller steps. Consistency in routines and structure can help children with ADHD to feel more secure and less overwhelmed.

Use positive reinforcement: Children with ADHD may struggle with impulsivity and hyperactivity, which can lead to negative behaviors. Using positive reinforcement can help to promote positive behaviors and improve self-esteem. This includes praising children for good behavior, setting rewards for good behavior, and providing opportunities for children to succeed.

Attention-deficit/hyperactivity disorder (ADHD) is characterized by symptoms such as difficulty maintaining attention, impulsivity, and hyperactivity. Managing ADHD symptoms can be challenging, and many individuals with ADHD struggle to navigate the demands of daily life, including school, work, and personal relationships.

ADHD coaching

ADHD coaching is a specialized form of coaching that is designed to help individuals with ADHD to manage their symptoms and improve their overall functioning. ADHD coaches work with clients to develop strategies and skills that can help them to better manage their symptoms and achieve their goals.

One of the key components of ADHD coaching is helping clients to develop strategies for organization and time management. Many individuals with ADHD struggle with disorganization, procrastination, and difficulty managing their time. A coach can help clients to develop strategies for breaking down tasks into smaller steps, setting priorities, and creating a schedule that works for them.

Another important aspect of ADHD coaching is working with clients to develop strategies for managing impulsivity and hyperactivity. This can include teaching clients mindfulness techniques, such as deep breathing and meditation, that can help them to stay focused and calm. Coaches can also work with clients to develop strategies for managing their physical activity, such as taking regular breaks and engaging in physical activity throughout the day.

In addition to these strategies, ADHD coaching can also focus on helping clients to improve their social and emotional well-being. Many individuals with ADHD struggle with social and emotional regulation, which can lead to difficulty in personal relationships. A coach can help clients to learn to communicate effectively, manage their emotions, and develop healthy relationships.

Coaching is an effective treatment for ADHD, and it can be used in conjunction with other forms of treatment, such as medication and therapy. It's important to note that ADHD coaching is not a substitute for medical treatment and it is important to work closely with a healthcare provider to develop an individualized treatment plan.

ADHD coaching can be done in person, over the phone, or even via video conferencing. It is important to find a coach who is trained and experienced in working with individuals with ADHD and who is able to provide a supportive and non-judgmental environment.

ADHD coaching is a specialized form of coaching that can help individuals with ADHD to better manage their symptoms and improve their overall functioning. It focuses on developing strategies for organization, time management, impulsivity, hyperactivity, and social and emotional regulation. It can be used in conjunction with other forms of treatment and can be done in person, over the phone, or via video conferencing. It is important to work closely with a healthcare provider to develop an individualized treatment plan that meets the unique needs of each individual.

What parents need to train their children

With the right approach, parents can help their children with ADHD learn to manage their symptoms and achieve success in their lives.

The first step in training children with ADHD is to understand the condition and its symptoms. ADHD is a neurobiological disorder that affects the brain's ability to regulate attention and behavior. Children with ADHD may have difficulty paying attention in class, following through on instructions, and controlling their impulses. They may also be easily distracted, fidgety, and impulsive.

The next step is to work with the child's healthcare provider and school team to create an individualized plan that addresses their specific needs. This may include medication, therapy, and accommodations in the classroom. Medication, such as stimulants, can help to improve attention and reduce impulsivity in some children with ADHD. However, it's important to note that medication should not be the only treatment and should be used in conjunction with other interventions.

Therapy can also be an effective treatment for children with ADHD. Behavioral therapy can help children learn new skills, such as how to pay attention, follow instructions, and control impulses. Family therapy can also be beneficial, as it can help parents and caregivers understand how to best support their children and manage their behavior.

In addition, parents can also make changes at home to help their child with ADHD. A structured routine can be helpful, as it can provide a sense of predictability and stability for the child. This can include consistent bedtimes and wake-up times, regular meal times, and a set schedule for homework and other activities.

It's also important to provide positive reinforcement for good behavior. This can include praising the child for staying on task, completing homework, or following instructions. Parents should also avoid criticizing or scolding the child for their ADHD symptoms, as this can lead to feelings of low self-esteem and further behavior problems.

Finally, parents should also educate themselves about ADHD and learn about the available resources. This can include attending support groups, talking to other parents of children with ADHD, and reading books and articles about the condition.

Training children with ADHD requires a comprehensive approach that addresses their specific needs. Parents should work with healthcare providers, school teams, and other professionals to create an individualized plan that includes medication, therapy, and accommodations. Additionally, parents can make changes at home, such as providing a structured routine and positive reinforcement, to help their child with ADHD learn to manage their symptoms and achieve success in their lives.

Implement behavior management techniques: Children with ADHD may benefit from behavior management techniques such as token economies, social stories, and self-monitoring.

These techniques can help children to learn appropriate behaviors and improve themselves.

EPILOGUE

Attention Deficit Hyperactivity Disorder (ADHD) is a complex condition that affects millions of children and adults worldwide. Managing ADHD can be challenging, but with the right strategies and support, individuals with ADHD can lead fulfilling lives. This book has provided an overview of ADHD, including the signs and symptoms, causes, and risk factors. It has also discussed various interventions and strategies that can help individuals with ADHD to manage their symptoms and improve their quality of life.

It is important to remember that every individual with ADHD is unique and may require a different combination of interventions to manage their symptoms. It's also crucial to understand that parenting a child with ADHD can be challenging, but with the right strategies, support and patience, parents can help their child to reach their full potential.

Managing ADHD can be challenging, but it is possible with the right support and understanding. With this knowledge, we hope that you have a better understanding of ADHD and the strategies that can help individuals with ADHD to lead fulfilling lives. Remember to always seek professional help and support, and never hesitate to reach out for help when needed.

www.ingramcontent.com/pod-product-compliance
Lightning Source LLC
Chambersburg PA
CBHW050806250726
48653CB00006B/2109